WHAT'S UP WITH WATER?

WHAT IS THE WATER CYCLE?

by Karen Latchana Kenney

Consultant: Marla Conn, Reading Specialist, Read-Ability

BEARPORT PUBLISHING

Minneapolis, Minnesota

Teaching Tips

Before Reading

- Look at the cover of the book. Discuss the picture and the title.
- Ask readers to brainstorm a list of what they already know about the water cycle. What can they expect to see in this book?
- Go on a picture walk, looking through the pictures to discuss vocabulary and make predictions about the text.

During Reading

- Read for purpose. Encourage readers to think about the water cycle and its role in life on Earth.
- Ask readers to look for the details of the story. What is happening during different parts of the water cycle?
- If readers encounter an unknown word, ask them to look at the sounds in the word. Then, ask them to look at the rest of the page. Are there any clues to help them understand?

After Reading

- Encourage readers to pick a buddy and reread the book together.
- Ask readers to name three things from this book that happen during the water cycle. Go back and find the pages that tell about these things.
- Ask readers to write and draw a picture of something that they learned about the water cycle.

Credits:
Cover, © Thomas Holt/Shutterstock and © ltummy/Shutterstock; Title page, © okawa somchai/Shutterstock; 3, © amenic181/iStock; 4, © patpitchaya/Shutterstock; 5, © RuudMorijn/iStock; 6, © robert_s/Shutterstock; 7, © konradlew/iStock; 8-9, © MarBom/iStock; 10–11, © Pictureguy/Shutterstock; 12, © mammuth/iStock; 13, © Blue Planet Studio/iStock; 15, © givaga/Shutterstock; 16, © Yuri Samsonov/Shutterstock; 17, © DenisTangneyJr/iStock; 18–19, © Kantapat/Dreamstime; 20, © CK Foto/Shutterstock; 21, © JTeivans/iStock; 22, © MicroOne/Shutterstock, © Anna Frajtova/Shutterstock, © Gor Grigoryan/Shutterstock, © Merkushev Vasiliy/Shutterstock; 23BL, © Dovzhykov Andriy/Shutterstock; 23BR, © Briedys/Dreamstime; 23TL, © Merkushev Vasiliy/Shutterstock; 23TR, © xxmmxx/iStock; 24, © CK Foto/Shutterstock

Library of Congress Cataloging-in-Publication Data

Names: Kenney, Karen Latchana, author.
Title: What is the water cycle? / Karen Latchana Kenney.
Description: Bearcub books. | Minneapolis, Minnesota: Bearport Publishing
Company, 2021. | Series: What's up with water? | Includes bibliographical references and index.
Identifiers: LCCN 2020030860 (print) | LCCN 2020030861 (ebook) | ISBN
9781647474928 (library binding) | ISBN 9781647474973 (paperback) | ISBN
9781647475024 (ebook)
Subjects: LCSH: Hydrologic cycle—Juvenile literature.
Classification: LCC GB848 .K46 2021 (print) | LCC GB848 (ebook) | DDC
551.48—dc23
LC record available at https://lccn.loc.gov/2020030860
LC ebook record available at https://lccn.loc.gov/2020030861

For more information, write to Bearport Publishing, 5357 Penn Avenue South, Minneapolis, MN 55419.

Printed in the United States of America.

Contents

Water on the Move!

Dark clouds fill the sky.

Drip, drip.

Rain starts to fall.

Later, the sun shines.

The **puddles** dry out.

Where did the water go?

The water went up to the sky.

Later, it will come down again.

Then, it goes back up.

This is the water **cycle**!

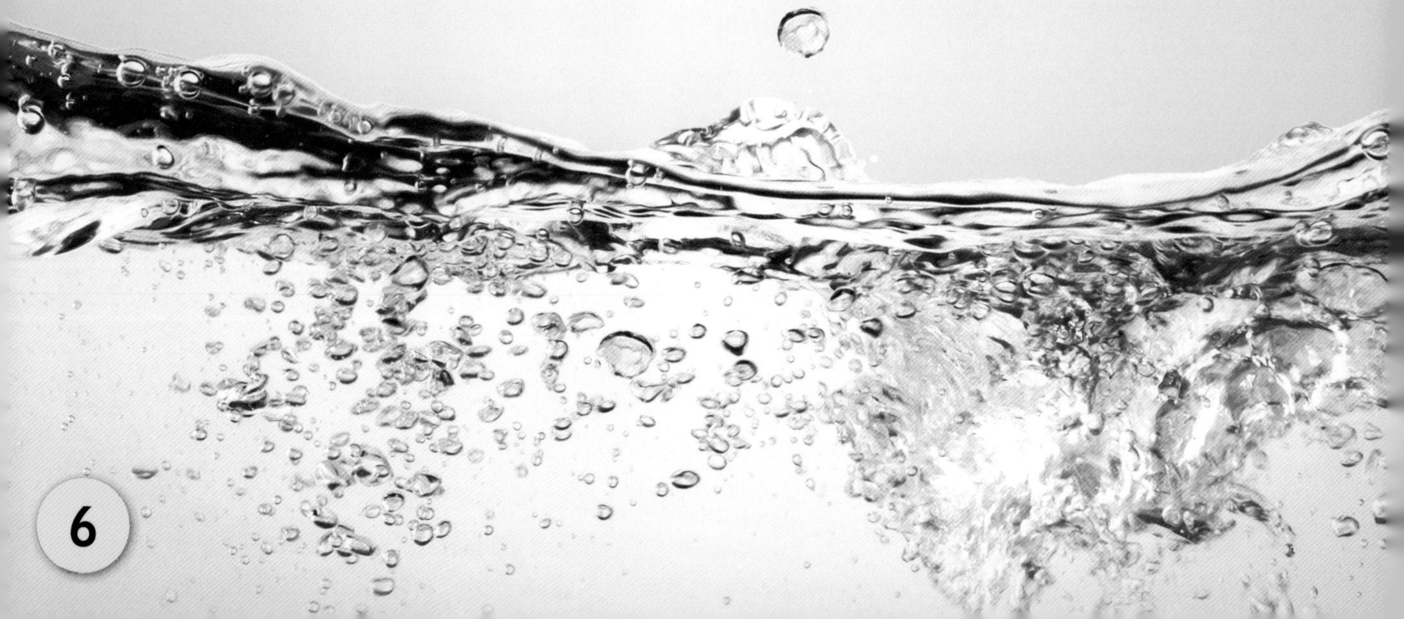

But how does water move?

Water **vapor** floats in the sky.

It is made of tiny drops of water.

The drops come together to make clouds.

Sometimes clouds fill up with too much water.

They need to let some go!

Then, water falls as rain or snow.

Water falls into oceans.

It falls on land and in lakes.

The water flows into rivers and streams.

Some sinks into the ground where plants pull it up.

Then, the sun shines down on Earth.

It heats up the land.

It heats up the lakes and oceans, too.

What happens to the water?

Heat turns water back into vapor.

Vapor rises up from the oceans, lakes, and streams.

It fills the sky.

Clouds **form** up high again.

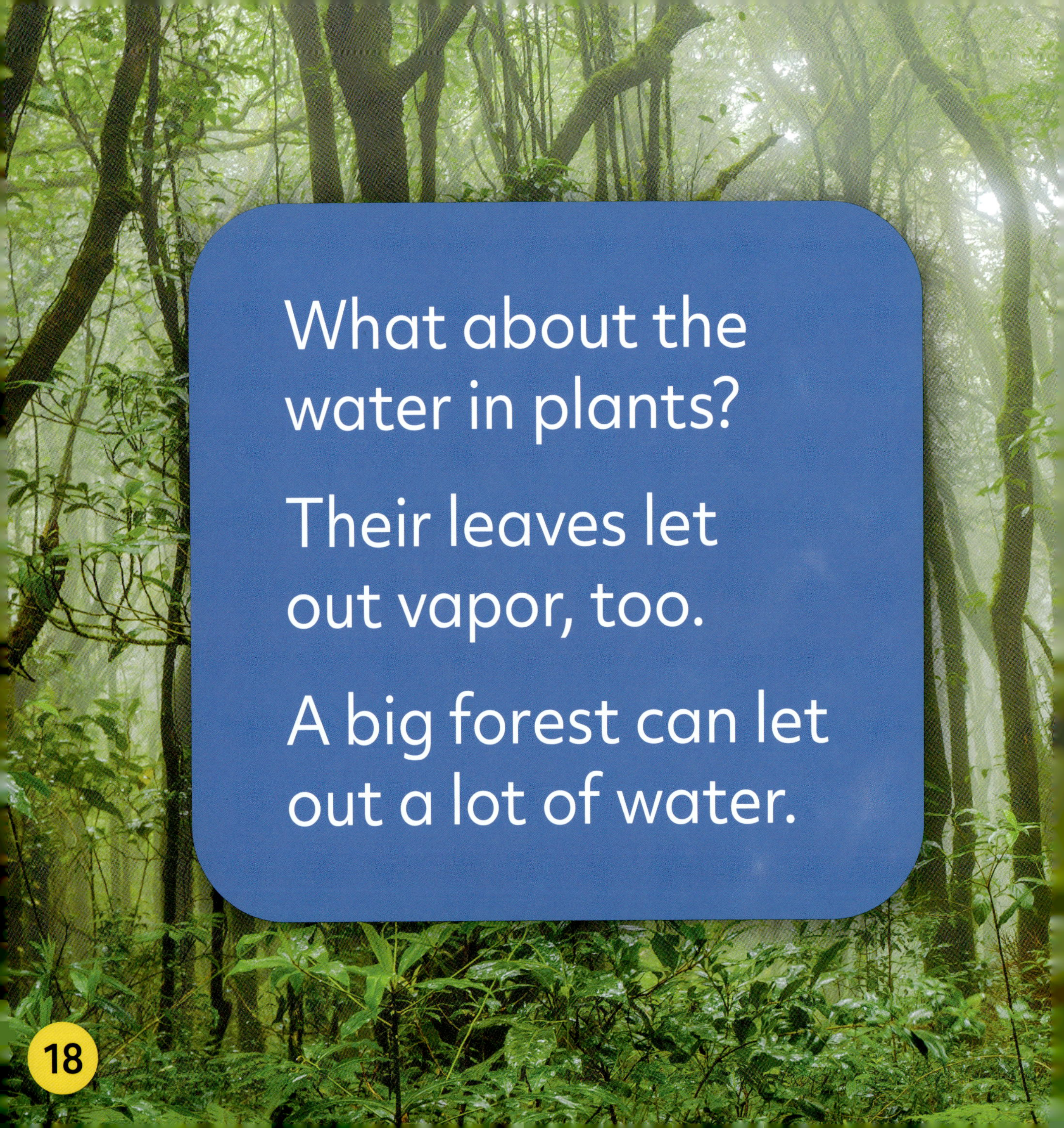

What about the water in plants?

Their leaves let out vapor, too.

A big forest can let out a lot of water.

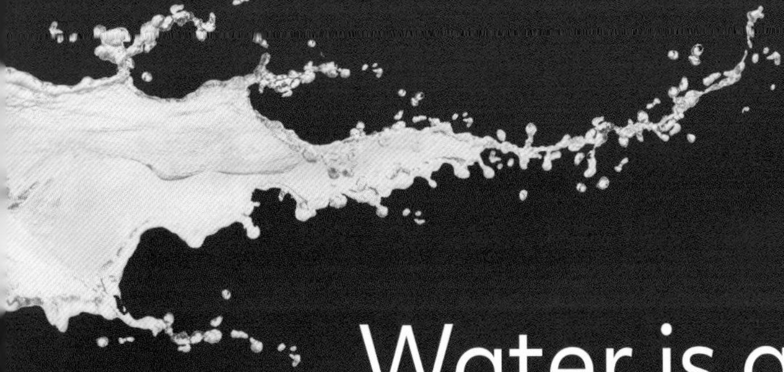

Water is always on the move.

Plants grow.

People have the food and water they need.

The water cycle helps all life on Earth!

The Water Cycle

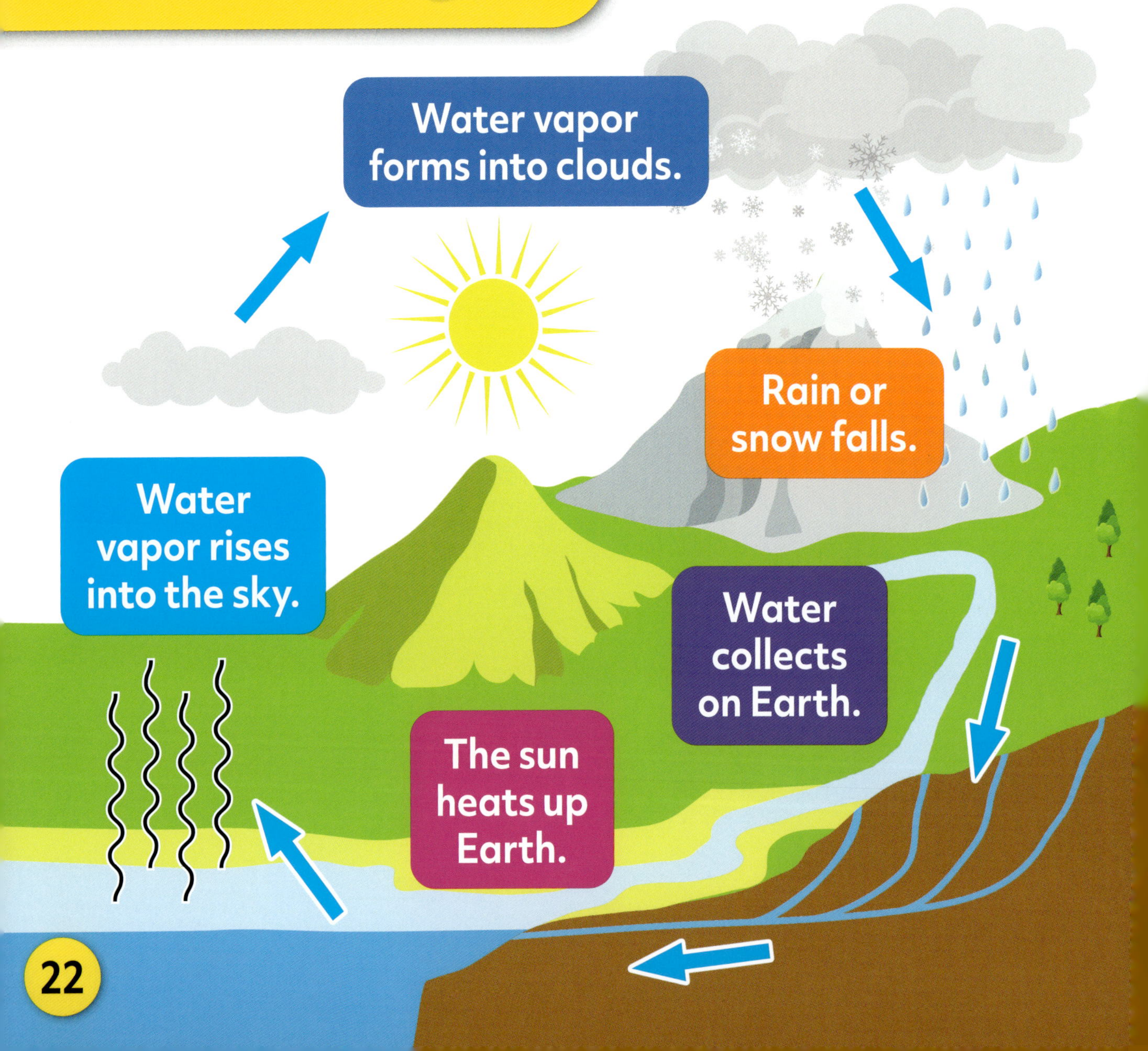

Glossary

cycle a series of events that repeat over and over

form to take shape

puddles tiny pools of water

vapor water in a gas form

Index

Read More

Moon, Emily Kate. *Drop: An Adventure through the Water Cycle.* New York: Dial Books for Young Readers, 2021.

Rogers, Marie. *Where Rain Comes From (Top-Secret Nature).* New York: PowerKids Press, 2021.

Learn More Online

1. Go to **www.factsurfer.com**
2. Enter "**Water Cycle**" into the search box.
3. Click on the cover of this book to see a list of websites.

About the Author

Karen Latchana Kenney writes and edits books about water, animals, and famous scientists. Born by the Amazon rain forest, she now lives in Minnesota.